Laughter: My Purgatory

For Bob,

Who is a good mentor
in the word-skills
of poetry.

Love

Paul

Laughter: My Purgatory

Br. Paul Quenon

Black Moss Press
2002

Published by Black Moss Press, 2450 Byng Road, Windsor, Ontario, Canada, N8W3E8.

Black Moss books are distributed by Firefly Books in Canada and the U.S.

Design by Karen Veryle Monck.

ISBN 0-88753-374-4

∾ TABLE OF CONTENTS

≈ CHICAGO

for Carl Sandburg

Such a tiny white box of a place,
with two front windows
lit by two red neon signs:
BUDWEISER   CHICAGO.
It bears the forlorn glamor,
in Marion County, Ky
of a big tough name
that once belonged to
this lonely village
where trains once stopped.
The railroad wouldn't allow
two Chicagos on one line
so its name was erased
and became Saint Francis.
Now the tracks too are erased
and the only trace of the past is
Chicago Tavern.
Set across from the Pizza Hut
that closed the year after it opened.
Chicago stays opened,
like Saint Francis church
which stands tall atop a knoll
with grass cut smooth all the way up
on every side. The town's sole pride
—about the only thing in sight
except for some cottages and
Chicago.

Nobody stops there,
unless they're from around here,
who go in and know everybody there
and hear their stories a dozen times over.
Stories like how Ted Mouser
shot himself shortly after
his 9th child was born
—and strange, him having been
in the monastery once—
and his wife still looking so young,
and him with his philosophical talk,
not even able to hold down a job,
like he'd rather be at home playing
with wife or kids
or having a drink.
And his brother too
left the monks and married
and ended up in prison
for running marijuana
to Chicago (the other one).
Then Ted's daughter grew to teen age
and made a suicide pact with two boys
and she alone survived, all blinded.
That was before their big house burnt down
'cause the youngest
turned the heater on
after Brother Martin told her not to
until he fixed it.
And the older boys got to selling pot,
were put in jail,
and another one stole a police car
to chase after his bride
who was running away. . .

Those who don't stop at Chicago
never hear these stories-
stories even Carl Sandburg would envy
of anybody who put them down in writing.
But nobody will.
They sound and fade away
within the wood frame walls
of Chicago.
And those who drive by
might smile if they've seen
that big brawny town.
They'd drive on
and assume such stories
are only heard in
Chicago.

∾ MY FIRST TONSURE

For Eileen 1940-1995

With primal awe I see sunlight
filter through her golden infant hair–
my play-pen companion and twin.
I desire, I reach with one fist
and hold. And holding with such an airy light
unaccountably pulls out a scream!
Mother bustles in, separates this goodness from me
and I feel wronged.

When her hair grew long and golden-curled
mine was dark and still infant short–
it seemed but mean destiny
until I learned mine too would grow long
if not cut.
So with new thought and tongue a little bit bolder
I whispered Mom to tell Dad not to cut it.

Haircutting day comes for all six of us,
the stool and the cloth and the clippers
are set up in the back yard.
With swift, jerking motions
clippers are passed across my entire scalp
and I know my desire is thwarted.
When released I run inside to the bedroom mirror
and see there a bald stranger
with a face sliding into contortion.

Today I gaze in the shaving mirror
at my bristled monk's head and think it
an odd prophecy of that a-religious man.
He liked the word Monk if not the idea,
and once in a story wrote ironically
of Monk: a gangster, growing old,
love-troubled, unsuccessful and self-doubtful.

As for her golden hair: it deepened in color,
changed shapes and shades,
and now in sudden darkness is vanished,
having become, with her,
pure light.

A CHANT FOR TRAPPIST AND DREPUNG LOSELING MONKS IN MAMMOTH CAVE

(On the occasion of the musical recording of Compassion, *with Millenia Music.)*

At the height of the solstice,
near the end of this millennium,
we descended deep into the darkness of the netherworld.

Down past a curtain of dripping water,
we retrace the footsteps of the slain Nazarene.

Behind us the iron gate slams shut with finality.
Somewhere a dog barks. The lock is turned:
"No one gets out," says the warden, "until everyone gets out."

With slow step we walk the dry flow
of a forgotten river,
where carved in stone
is a secret music
more ancient than humanity.
With flute, cello and low murmured chant,
we approach the caverns of Pluto,
where, with voice and lyre,
Orpheus enchanted
his forbidden entry.

Here the ratios and proportions of music
are reduced to their elementary nature.

Here, bow stroked string
with such feather touch, that the
harmonic cut the fibre to a shred.
Here, sound, born of silence,
snapped the string that awakened it,
for all begins in chaos.

Here the high cheeked natives once gathered by firelight,
where deepest drone of high cheeked Asians
now release crystal overtones that roll
free in the vault of the quartz ceiling.

Here my breathless Alleluias, in triple ascent,
fail to attain God, until
with bottomless tones you, my Buddist brothers, rise up
in measured gradation, and complete some obscure
code of sound and meaning.

Here have we come, because the unchanging truth is
that all things change,
–even death.

And "Your music alone, O god with the lyre,
soars eternal."

For music is quick
and subtle enough alone to say:
nothing is permanent.

Here we have come,
monks with memories more ancient
than any government or state,
to find the visage of a forgotten humanity.

Is ours to be the tragedy of Orpheus
to recover, then lose, the face we love
for desiring to see it too soon?

Or will ours it be
to ascend and gaze toward the light,
and show the face of that Resurrection?

Here we come at the uncertain turn
of a new millennia,
where no darkness is so absolute,
no temple so ancient,
no silence so deep,
to sow a harvest of prayers
of peace and compassion.

Meanwhile, someone has cheated the warden,
escaped already,
and is preparing a banquet above.

≈ MEDITATION METHOD

Listening to concert
people sit
            very still.
The music speeds up
we listen the more
and sit
            very still.
The faster it goes,
the less we move;
the rhythm pulls tighter
the lines move swifter,
in legato ascends.
Holding tighter, I sit faster
break into
double time, I hear the cello
echo in counter time
as I sit stiller
and move faster.

A deaf man enters the room
wonders at all the people
there
who are gone.
Nowhere gone, because
they are there.
They sit and stare, and see not
as though they were elsewhere;
Each moment might never end
or any moment suddenly break
into an avalanche –
but does not.

They stay still
and forget time is passing.

Time has forgotten them;
is blind to heads leaning,
sitting very still,
still as a nun before dawn
forgetting the dark,
for this melody moves in light,
banks and turns and dives;
a circle of swallows
skating on air,
leaving, returning,
crossing the high arena,
blind to listeners sitting very still
in the semi-dark of a concert hall.

The deaf man turns and leaves,
senseless of how so many people
are a single winged creature
soaring on an updraft,
cresting in golden air
towards an unlimited horizon.

≈ NO SOUND

No sound from the moon.
Only drops falling from eaves
On dry winter leaves,

'til over the hill
a dog fills his own echo,
barking at his barks.

I do not notice
when he stops. Only my thoughts
are silent again.

∼ THAT TIME AT CANA

We thought it was a joke
—a kind of wicked joke—
just when spirits were high
and the vats low
I was supposed to
pour water into the goblets!

As good as telling everyone to go home.

"Do whatever he tells you,"
says the strange lady. . .
The quiet young man
seemed as annoyed as I, at first.

But the boys and I got to laughing
—we couldn't help it—
and went ahead and just did whatever he told us.

Even the bridegroom seemed
in on it all:
when he tasted the cup
his eyes lit up!

After so much cheap wine
plain old water tastes so good!

But guests started gathering around . . .

It was too curious, and I stole a taste.
That's when the sobriety hit me.

I was afraid

–didn't say anything.

The boys started talking.
Guests decided they had been drinking on the side
and had taken to telling wild stories.

Then I got blamed.

"It came straight out of the well," they said,
and the more they protested
the funnier it got,
Oh! What an evening! I thought there would
never be an end to it all.

To this day there hasn't been.

I tell you,
I would trade my soul
for one more taste of that drink:

its bouquet of paradise,
rich, full bodied as blood,
subtle as that strange woman's smile,
exhilarating as the laughter of angels.

≋ SILK SCREEN

I see, in my dream,
an ancient silk screen:
a budda seated
by a scrub pine,
with a pile of cones.

The inscription:
"For a thousand years
I have sought enlightenment.
All that has resulted
is this little brown cluster
of cones.

Even that is getting smaller."

~ ORACLES OF A BEDRIDDEN MONK

Would somebody come and wake me up?

> *

Are we going to do some yelling?
Are we going to do some praying?
- or both?

> *

Dear Jesus
Dear Jesus
Dear Jesus

Come on, come on, come on.

Dear Jesus
Dear Jesus

Come on, com'on, com' on.

Dear Jesus
Hurry up, hurry up, hurry up
com'on, com'on.

You can save me better than that!

> *

I wanna go
I wanna go
I wanna go to that place

I wanna
            GO
to that place
Where do all the people wanna go?

Where do all the people
            wanna go?
Where do
            all the people

            go?

They go to another place.
They all go to another place.

All the people go
            to another place.

Where do they go to give stamps?
Where do they go to give
            stamps?

They go where they can be homesick.
They wanna go where they can be
                        homesick
                                    sick

                                    sick

Did we get any card?
No, no.
Did we get any card
            up here?
No, no, no.

Did we get any card
down?

Did you see any cards floating by?
No, no, no.

Did you see any yellow cards floating by
                              by
                                    by?

*

Gamble, gamble, gamble
      Who wants to gamble?

*

The night, the night;
I dread the night!
I don't know why.
I dread it like anything.

*

I have something to ask you.
Is that O.K.?
Now listen to me very carefully.
You don't need to have 10 Masses said for me.
Just say one Mass for me

—and skip the ceremonies.

Is that O.K.?

*

Angus, Angus!
May God love and bless you
and put you where you can continue
all the good works you are doing,
until he takes you up to heaven
where we will rejoice
with all the saints and angels.
I thank you.
O.K.? O.K.?

I've got to keep quiet.
I'm making too much noise.

≈ NINE HAIKU

From frog-eye level
a comment on the world comes
at evening: Ge-lump!

Big, still moon above
Deep in my coffee mug swims
small shimmering moon.

Moonshine shivering
dancing in my mug, tastes
to me just like coffee!

In the morning dark
I sense some deer are present-
a bare suspicion.

It's not the winter.
No, the crows' raucous revels
drive all the birds south.

Huddled in my coat
I hear the blue jay sass me:
"I love this spring cold."

The Mockingbird calls,
morn 'till noon, then quits. His sort
of understatement.

Old monk sets out
to meditate. He ends up
imitating cows.

Water, shadow, shale
Eon after long eon
they mutter haiku.

≈ HICKORY DEATH

Church cliff
pig-nut
rock rooted
prostrates
core snapped
wind felled
at church cliff.

Monks' graves
held roots
death deep
100 years.

Thund'rous trunk
core snapped
lies felled.

Church rock
not moved
not moved
very far.

❧ FOR EILEEN 1940-1995

I dream you are alive –
young, healthy, real as daylight.
We're in the garden.

"I thought you were dead!
Why simulate death and leave?
Were you with some man?"

She is mute, then says:
"He is a kind of healer.
They say he once died."

My alarm wakes me
to dark. To reality's
hard, opaque, sad dream.

❧ GRAMMAMACHIA:
THE BATTLE OF THE LETTERS

The letters one day held discussion
   on that nebulous old word: the page.
It's a word they had heard, not something they'd seen.
So it'd lost repercussions
   of a more religious age.

The fact of its lessened recurrence
   made some letters feel quite appalled.
While others, bemused or indifferent,
   bemoaned its recurrence at all.

"I don't see this page you speak of,
   there's nothing of it you can show.
Without any lines or position
   just how could we possibly know?

Unless you can give it description
   it's best to abandon the word.
It's so like us silly letters
   to spell out a thought that's absurd."

Claimed the I: "Its dimensions are vertical."
   Claimed the T: "Its dimensions are two."
The dash disagreed, but the dot made a plea
   "With dimensions it has nothing to do."

The Y said "It brings both together."
   The C said, "It's neither to me."
The S on the question did waver.
   while the X crossed it off of the chart.

The O said "It adds up to zero."
   The question mark said: "Just who knows?"
The K said, "It's surely assertive
   with lines that march like a Kraut.

The mystical Q said "It is round,
   with a serpent that crawls inward or out."
The A called it all, the Z named it zilch.
   The comma gave pause to consider the cause.
Said the colon: "I don't give a turd."

They busied themselves on the issue,
   were pulling it all quite apart.
They shredded it down to a tissue,
      then declared their rhetoric art.

And while there was no resolution
the question had scarcely evolved –
the words multiplied
where these letters reside,
   and the page would provide
   no solution.

For the page in a spirit of game
has its own rather secretive aim.
Should the argument end
it would empty stand then
and the page really likes convolutions.

∾ MEDLEY OF THE ENTRANCED

Strike the travesty in
  two enamored masks
confessing heartbreak
with round blue lips.

Oh sincere purple lips:
I tried, I tried: 491-9573
  and there was
No Answer: not even
  a medley of deception.
So I hung up, and
The Tape Loop snapped.

What remains is no Remainder.
No Placid Sea without
a Shadow, no rapid Swell of
a Deep Shadow.

No apology.

Try again
if you must.

Strike the travesty . . .

ॐ TENDERLY

a recording by Oscar Peterson

Report the ancient night, Oh, guess her changing air
Dress her in quick silks,

down tripper
solemn angel – candy child

                  coy outside in, - genius inside out
Golden-haired star on celluloid desire.

Oh tell like it is – that only breeze –
        Yeaaa, like it isszzz
-zz, whisper, half-say, tenderly.

Flash like stars of crystal streetlights
  –treble cry of evening breeze.

Stay you soft
       and, Oh dash off Oscar to thump of bass

come on cat feet

make like one acrobatic cat on his day off

Joy Kid here
scissor switch there, toe lick double stitch
god, I wanna swear!

(That's what rhythm comes from, kid!)

Tell it tender, caress my ease   and it
  don't sit here, and it don't sit there
          Swiss witch tickle-tock
           weave a stitch diamond clock

down
        the daylight valley of the breeze GO
           two, three, four

        The ev'ning fleas tickle my knees
        cwy, cwy, cradle lee be-be

Send a fury WHIRL, deliver that BREAK

Chord – columns – climb where angels fear to play
                              masquerade
in some devil vaudeville
                  tap pat tap nice old Goody Two-Shoes
                     in kindergarten day
Oh, but nail it down Daddy! then let it float away

Send it down the city till it hits all ports
                              Yea, roll it!
This little mean tiger is gonna have his day –
                              Like now!
Twenty longshoremen
        Twenty longshoremen went to the town of New York
      glimmer'n shadow, glimmer'n shadow, flatt-er
        FLEE the licky-click girl!

Don't mess with me, baby
        I'm king of mud-basin blues.
Finger crunch bunny, I get mean –

–I mean, ease it up Sarah so
the air o'night   comes

            all tinkly pinwheel down.

Dark flows the spreading night hair.

≈ NOVEMBER CUTTINGS

Each dry plant sounds unique.

Basil cutting shiver
and leak high pixie sqeaks.
Prickly sweetness gets released:
a citrus – rose-hip – frost- sing
subtle as innocense.

Saliva stalks sough drab
and quit without a song.

Laurel politely chatters
like death never was
and the party only gets better
every year.

One squat juniper,
topped by wind,
deeply clutches earth
and pokes a jagged accusation
at the sky.

∽ EMINENT EXPLETIVES

Balderdash is the name of a dog.
Malarkey is the name of a parrot.
Falderol is the word Demosthenes practiced
        With a pebble in his mouth.

Balderdash is a sauce for cornbeef and cabbage.
Malarkey is a county in Ireland.
Falderol is an architectural conceit on a
        Renaissance palace.

Balderdash is the cud of a camel.
Malarkey is a rare species of kangaroo.
Falderol is a wrestling foul.

Fiddle-faddle is the tangle in a yarn basket.

Balderdash is an additive for marijuana.
Malarkey is a minor Hebrew prophet.
Falderol is the name of a boa constrictor.

Bull shit is only what it says.

～ MY FIRST SIN

The half dome of our house yard
slopes into blackness. Random
points of light move
and vanish in the air.
I'm told they are alive and
my sister names them for the first time.

And I think: How are lightning-bugs caused by lighting?

"Here. They wouldn't hurt you, hold it in your hand."

The spaces between my fingers light up a cool green
and disappear. Yet the thing does not go away
and lights another corner of my hand.

"Let's catch and put them in a jar."

And the night becomes a wild dance of frustration
and random luck. The jelly jar
becomes not the loaded bank I want,
but does crowd with light when shaken once,
twice, but not a third or fourth time.

"See, if you tear it out the lighter stays lit.
You can smear it on your skin too."

When morning comes Mother asks:
"What happened to the jar of lighting bugs last night?"

"We threw them into the commode, turned off the light,
flushed and they spinned around
faster and faster."

"Oh honey, don't do that. . ."

"But it's pretty!"

⌇ SNAPSHOTS OF MOM

She brushed her hair, bunched the strands
        and tossed them out the window
        for the birds to make a nest.

Favorite swear word: "O Jerusalem!"

I asked what they were fighting about in World War I.
        She gazed off with face blank, lifted her shoulders and
        let them drop. I thought it was ignorance or something
        completely beyond her. Since then I have read many histo-
ries- I now regard it as wisdom.

Gray at 45, a tuft still black concealed at the nape of her neck:
        "I had raven hair."

In High School she had to write a story
and read it to the class:
        "My story was about this girl
who takes something from her
        boy friend.
He tries to find it, and – Oh, I was so
embarrassed
 – all the boys laughed when I got to a line that
        said: "He crept into her room and searched through her
        drawers. . ."

Best meal: fried chicken, green beans,
and mashed potatoes,
        Sunday afternoons, invariably.

"What did the Reverend Monseigneur say at Mass today?" She
replies:
"Whereas. . . of course. . . therefore. . . in so far as. . ."

Learning to drive at 52:
            a car opposite makes a left and collides.
            My brother out of the car
and talking to the driver;
            she behind the wheel, her foot
still pressing the brake.

Returning home late at night, the end
after months of visits to
            Dad in the hospital:
            I hear calming voices,
            hers rising above:
            "I didn't want that to happen!
            "I didn't want that to happen!"

Settled in a new house, near relatives again:
            My brother stops by
on the way home from the coal mine:
            "How are you?"
            She sits down on a stool: "Sometimes I can hardly keep
going." – I had thought everything was fine.

Friday nights sitting with her friend Rachel
in front of the TV, glasses of beer in hand,
watching the boxing matches, which came after

"I Remember Momma."

After school I found her sitting
 in a dark corner of the church vestibule:
  "Are you all right?" "I'm thinking of what to buy for Christmas
while in town."

To the Sodality ladies:
          "I can always tell when my son is home from High School –
          crash, bam, slam . . . "

"The day your Aunt Katherine was married we carried her down Main
street in Farmington in a wheelbarow. "

"Your Dad said the first time he saw me
          he was on the jitney riding past home and saw me
          coming down the front steps.
          He said to himself:
          'That's the girl I'm going to marry."

Driving through the country we come upon a hay field being
harvested.
          "O, now that's what I consider really beautiful!"
          –the windrows curving, dark and light along the contours of
          the hills.

I, in my Trappist habit, speaking alone with her:
          Her question left me speechless:
          "Do you have faith?"

Another one of her children leaves the Church:
          "What will she do? – out completely and left with nothing!"
Her upturned palm drops to her side.

Her first child died an infant.
>"I believe Jacky went to heaven and became an angel."
>Years later, she continued counting birthdays.

At 75, holding an infant when my Aunt arrives:
>"Don't worry, Ethel, this one's not mine."

Always healthy until that terminal heart condition:
>"I've never had anything before, only colds. . . and babies."

Last visit home:
>"That garage down from the church burnt to the ground.   It
>used to be a chapel
where your father and I were married."

Last phone call home, her voice much weaker.
>I try to revive her with enthusiasm and interest.
>She is swept back, loses the effort.
 Aunt Francis takes the phone.

☙ UNWORKING DEFINITIONS OF OBSCURE WORDS

FIB' – U – LA; n.
>   The invertebrate habit of telling fibs,
>   or, the indisposition consequent upon telling a fib.
>   Or, the little bone where untold fibs hide
>   and if you look it up in a dictionary it is
>   because you think I'm fibulating.

UN- CAN' – NY: adj.
>   i.e. Unassociated with cans
>   or anything inside them
>   as these are prosaic and everywhere found
>   even in Warhol paintings
>
>   and are ignored until opened
>   and discarded when empty
>   into a can for cans
>   which in turn is emptied
>   and is ignored until filled
>
>   unlike the uncanny
>   which is full when empty
>   and is ignored always and rarely mentioned
>   except as trashy language
>   or from high pulpits
>   where it is mostly
>   canned, preprocessed, and then
>   ignored even more-
>   odorless, tasteless and vacuum sealed.

Only when punctured,
>when with a hiss
>>the uncanny rushes in
is its subtle aroma at last
>you might say
uncanned.

CON'- FLU- ENCE n.
>As when the community, together, gets the flu.

>The influence of con men.

>When crows fly together and make great raucous
>in a spot to which
>they flew,
>they're in confluence.

OS- TEN-TA'- TION; n.
>Sweeping wide his arms with "O",
>in a Ten Gallon Stetson,
>polysyllabic ostentation
>steps forth with a voice
>stentorian,
>riddles us flat with a triple "T",
>as he takes his station
>on the state of the nation:

>"It's not like it was in Austin."

>The ladies say: "Gracious!"
>How ostentatious!"

RE-BAR-BA-TIVE: adj.
    Barbed repeatedly.

    St. Sebastian, with arrows shot
    bristled splendidly
    all tied back
    refusing to die
    just to vex
    smooth pagans
    who barbered obsessively
    every inch of their skin.
    These never won such fame
    as spikely old Sebast
    who alone is allowed in church
    with a loincloth on

–besides Jesus, that is.

PRAT'- TLE v.
    To chatter on
    spout and splatter,
    and rattle like a car
    that rambles and clatters
    with nowhere to go
    because the talking head inside
    has no one in the driver's seat.

E'- BUL'- LIENCE   n.
    as bouillon
    when brought to a boil

or a bull when piqued
gave chase to acrobat
boys at Samothrace
who with joy
and consummate grace
flipped to a peak
and there
where frozen in space
on an ancient vase
set in a chamber
deep in the Met.

Ebullience
stilled– still leaping the span
of time and space.

∿ THE RIDDLE

By Thomas Merton

I might be defined
The imaginative kind.
My life is charmed,
Untouched by harm.

Fast or slow
Off I go
To view the scene
On cloud serene.

What secret I've read
I leave unsaid;
It'd make you smile,
Or puzzle awhile.

My naked heart
Betrays no art,
With nothing concealed,
And nothing to steal,

Nothing to know
Nothing to dream;
I tell no lies.
In truth, my eyes

Are globes that see
All lands and seas:
I never complain
Be it China or Spain.

I've been around
And always found
Great happiness,
Tremendous bliss.

At earth's deep core
I've seen no sore . . .
And if I fly
To spheres on high,

Or visit afar
Some secret star
In depths of night
Though quite profound

–to put it right–
I would be found
To be
No one and everyone.

When I fly free
Of memory,
You should not yearn
For my return,

Or try to see
Where I might be.
I'm there, unknown;
In nothing shown.

Without a face,
Without a name,
Without renown
Or any fame.

I am a strange
Enchanted bird:
God formed me – Love,
By his own word.

Translations of Le Secret

From The Collected Poems of Thomas Merton.

A New Directions Book. Pg. 635.

≈ ULTIMATE MORALITY

If I desire the cessation of desire,
I still desire. To try as I may
to end it all is still to try.

Tried by life, with pistol to my head,
I try back with
one last shot
and down I go, lost to being tried
by my own trying.

What illusory self began this desire?
I canonize my craze for ultimate autonomy
by a kamikaze lunge,
offering everything to the idol of
the wanting I.

The Buddha never wanted nirvana.
Saints have quit the hell of wanting heaven.

≈ BY THE HEARTH

Daughter: That sound in the fire –
like voices chatting –
What is that?

Father: It's the fire-people.
They've awakened
and talk – talk of the towers
and castles of flame
rising tall around them.

Daughter: How'd they get there?

Father: They came down on a sunbeam
and were locked in the wood
many years ago.

Daughter: I hear a low Grandfather growl!
And a whistle and a pop– what's that?

Father: It's a cold moonbeam
getting out of there
as fast as it can.

❧ THE BOTTOM LINE IS

I'll not stand for
how you always draw your bottom line
an inch above me.
I'm through towing the line
on a bottom that gets yanked out from under me
every time the bottom line of
everything you're above doing
becomes
the bottom line of everything I've already done.
Like you've kicked the bottom out –
there's no where to go but
down,
so low
not even Satan can draw
the bottom line that is me
landed flat on my face
where you can walk all over me
and make ME your definition of

the bottom line.

∼ THANKSGIVING, OR
ALL BIRDS' DAY

for Bob Hill

Already we'd seen a marsh hawk coasting low and limber above dry
brush frosted sage and blue. Thanksgiving Day and we stopped on
back roads, clambered over bridges, me fixated by the XXXX of steel
girders, the solemn dark of water, reversal of reflected tree forms.

We stop at the Byrd's home, where pet ostriches leer down with flash-
ing eyes and pass imperious judgement. Lumpish claws, like E.T.
grown arthritic, 60 mph speed limit. Faces are eyes on the end of a
neck, hair sticking out from ears. Soon America will package them in
football loafs, same as turkeys tasting generic like anything you might
want for whatever occasion.

We head off to a house we can't find of a friend who isn't home. So
we sip Coors by the coots' lake where killdeer freely flock, bottoms
tilted white, flutter low – when a hawk closes in, strikes, pushes one
down in the water and returns to a tree. Cooper's Hawk. Nothing
but one feather visible on the water, not one killdeer in sight. Such
primal competition before our unbelieving eyes! Over corn fritters
left by casual parkers.

So went the day of birds, and – Oh yes – even the night when in a
dream I heard: "Let us begin, let us begin," speech translated as I
awoke into sound of a modest "who-who-de-who" of the owl.

∾ SKETCHES OF GRANDMOTHER

I

Saying little, she sits very still, listening. So frail, she
sits as the slightest movement of her frame begins, a rhythm with
the head nodding in assent, in the rate of the heartbeat nodding,
ceasing and beginning, continuing on, nodding in assent to the
world as it is.

How could so many hills and curves fit within one face? As if the
whole globe was there made small. One skin feature prominent,
round, is called, I'm told, a mole– something that
old people get.
Named and so diagnosed, it seemed an ordinary face after
all.

At Grandmother's were copies of LIFE,
with big pictures from all around the world–
big and puzzling, telling of the war
and things that came over the radio.
Sometimes pictures of
"the firemen's parade" she called it,
meaning nudes on the ceiling of the Sistine.
Meanwhile futilely I searched back and forth
for some kind of parade.

Alone on the porch she suddenly gives way to laughter, repeated and
prolonged, teasing and fussing,
with no company in view.
I rush out the door in time to see a chipmunk spin and
disappear,afraid of me but not of her.

At the end of a visit, amidst good-bys, kisses, and smiles, she project
towards the kids her false teeth.
I take it as a special grandmother's smile, bigger than the other
grown-ups if not very pretty.

Leaning over the porch railing at nightfall, a conversation
begins I've heard before. Aunt Madeline says to her:
       "It's about time for you to go to bed."
       "Well, don't forget to lock the door."
       "Why should I lock the door?"
       "A darkie might come in and carry me off."
       "Listen to that! Eighty-two years old and still thinking
anyone would carry her off!"

Whenever my sister and I left the house to go downtown – downtown
was a whole block and a half long – we were reminded:
       "Don't let the darkies grab you."
I imagined that was some private bogey of hers.
No one in that town
fit the description.

II

My oldest brother kneels by her chair with a camera:
       "Can I take your picture Grandmother?"
Weeks later, the result:
She looks out astonished
delicate, poised
eyes deep and full
ancient yet timeless
astonished perhaps at her own offspring in the bloom of manhood,
astonished at the word as it is.

In the same room a portrait of Pius XII,
erect, lean, looking out,
sitting as if forever, the white ermine embroidery
running vertical on the front of his red velvet coat,
sitting alert in a world where all is in revolution,
seated as if chaos did not exist, as Abraham Lincoln sat,
as Whister's Mother,
as if there were no other reality than this frame on a wall
facing a portrait on the wall opposite
of the venerable Bishop in the seat of an obscure
mountain diocese, and between them
Anna Deveny Hagerty real and alive,
tending the house with her quiet,
where the noise of six children grown has withdrawn,
where noise will come of grandchildren,
and children of theirs;
her rosary nearby at rest
sitting with her thoughts, or with no thoughts
with no heaviness, nor lightness
not willing to be, nor unwillingly to be
as if no other activity were in creation,
and creation were this being
on this chair, in this room, in a house
on a hillside across from the Methodist Church
in a coal town in West Virginia.

Later I found the photograph in the trash.
        "Mom, what is it doing in here?"
        "Oh, it makes her look so old . . ."

⚈ DECODING A DREAM

Before birth I was one.

At my birth I was divided into two,
        and the half that is me lived.
        the half that was me lived also,

though I wondered it could survive
        the separation.

Between us was stitched
        a code of conduct and a boundary of custom
that kept us two and kept us together.

My spirit revolted against this boundary
        and plotted to restore to the one.
But in all of creation there was no assistance found,
        and the order of things to me
        was dumb
        and I forgot.

This page is a confession I have not given up
although I know not what I'm doing.

The harder I try to return to the other
        the more obstacles I find
        the more structures I climb

and the well remembered way
        grows longer.

My trek to the heights
ends back in school
where the teachers are kind
            but the hour of time
            seems off-center.

I seek a forbidden pleasure
            which for me is the measure
            of all I have ever done.

            Can I ever be one?

Must my secret desire
            forever be dumb?
(I can't explain it myself!
            -but dream it I do)

            and you?

≈ KATYDIDS

Katydid racket
slaps the ear,
tears the night,
and rags the air

with itch and passion.

Katydids saw and rachet
from massive
black
rows
of gum trees.

They bracket the road,
sass and splatter.

Row against row
they echo back,
then clap,
mirac'

      lous- ly

           clap
a unanimous clap

then slip right back
to the reckless thrash of
one gigantic all night
     bash.

∽ MERTON CAMPUS

Sleeping before the fireplace on the hermitage floor,
I dream kittens are on the porch
Where I had left cheese scraps after dark.
Friendly, they crawl over me.

I walk here in a future time.
A residency hall stands where the juniper was.
A meditation group of some oriental practice is arriving.
A woman with dark eyes looks deeply into mine,
as though she knows me,
and I must recognize their teacher's name.
But I am behind the times
and have fallen ignorant.

The grove on the east has become a sprawling university.
Where the maple stood, a tower rises.
Soap suds fill an apartment
being purified. A student died there of AIDS.
Suds drift from the window and wet my shirt.

I wake. The ground is covered with snow.
The cheese is gone.

For Vigils, II Nocturne, I read of early Irish solitaries
– gealta, "volatiles" —
who stood in icy streams and prayed;
battle scarred warriors, atoning for the slain.
"Brother Drycthelm, it is amazing you can endure
such bitter cold!"
He growls back: "I've seen far worse."
A geilt lived in trees, fed on grass, on watercress;
might grow feathers, and could fly.

At dawn I walk to the juniper
where the dream apartment was.
Birds gather there.
In the snow, two big melt spots
where two bodies slept,
dog tracks or coyote there — whatever.
I thank the grateful cheese lover
who sent me that friendly dream
from the front porch.
I step carefully through briers,
advancing toward the sun,
the old paths blocked by snow-felled trees.
The road now washes into a rocky rivulet.
There a sign for rare travelers
is nailed to a tree, half faded.
I peer closer: "Watch out
for pedestrians, 8-10 a.m."
—Father Kelty's rye remark to gunmen.
The old trukey"Geilty" wades the cold stream here
everyday.

I jump it to a field:
streaked green and white:
campus, campi.
The sun holds forth above
on a pyramid of light rays.
Quickly I turn away,
too clever, too educated,
for such elementary
brilliance.

Hand over hand, I pull myself
up a wooded bank to a clearing
marked by more melt spots:
guts & blood there, pink and scat brown.
Something born here
or something slain. Dog tracks.
Snow feathered clear
as by a large wing.

The University Of The Campus . . .

I pass the vacant mound where the Boone house was,
the barn now removed. A pine lot growing.
100 years ago this was a girl's school.

Paths I once could walk are overgrown with thickets.

All human traces disappear.
Nature holds to its ways.

Lesson ended.

≈ A NIGHT VISITOR

A grey clowd cover
hides the moon, blanketing light
as night grows lonely.

My ears are stifled
by the crush of my own thoughts
'til silence says: Hush.

These ears are windows
opening on quiet night
where my soul can breathe.

If I could reach out
to touch this fragile silence
she would shy away.

She offers presence,
not familiarity,
to my calloused hand.

Close as my own breath,
though my mind be far away,
precious as a prayer.

Rare is the moment
when, with nothing on my mind,
I hear her passage,

subtle as a sigh.